D1014699

Purple Ronnie's Little Book of Chocolate

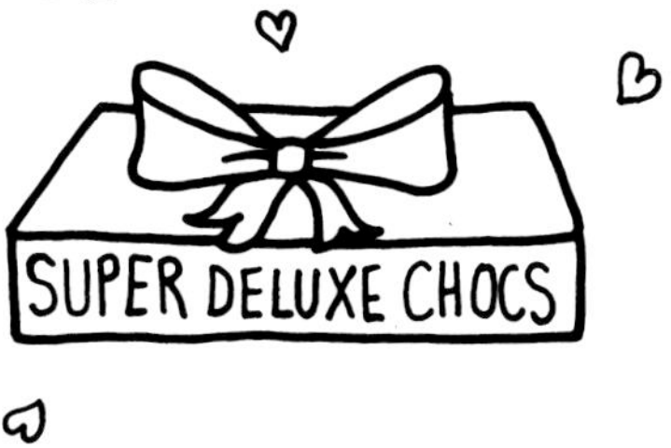
SUPER DELUXE CHOCS

by Purple Ronnie

First published 2005 by Boxtree
an imprint of PanMacmillan Publishers Ltd
20 New Wharf Road
London N1 9RR

www.panmacmillan.com

Associated companies throughout the world

ISBN 0 7522 2563 4

9 8 7 6 5 4 3 2 1

A CIP catalogue record for this book is
available from the British Library

Text by Giles Andreae
Illustrations by Janet Cronin
Printed and Bound in Hong Kong

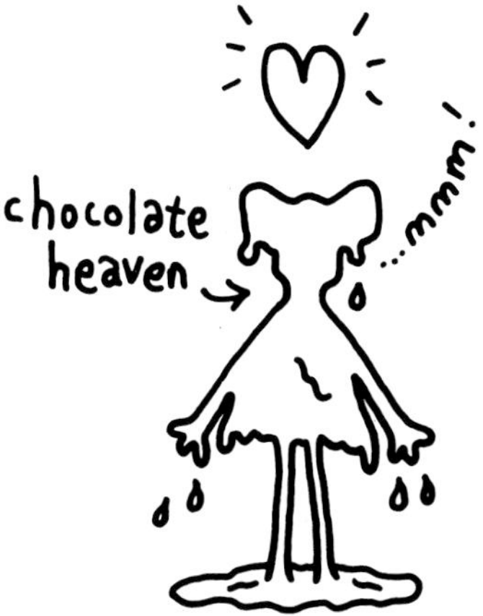
chocolate heaven
...mmm!

a poem for a
Chocolate Lover

Whether life seems full
of joy

Or whether life seems
crappy

A little bit of chocolate

Can always make you
happy!

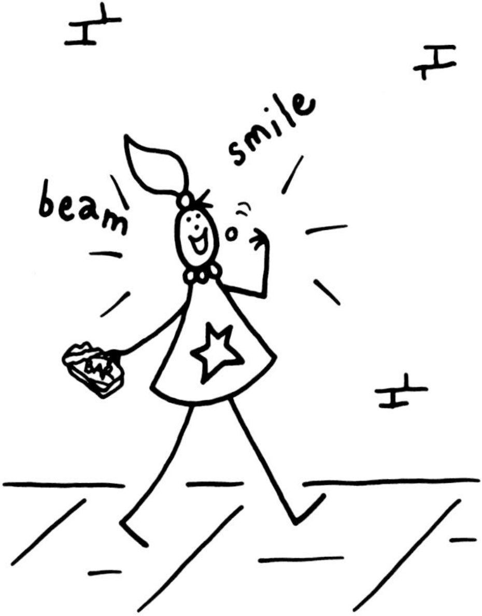
beam
smile

Interesting Fact

Chocolate often tastes nicer when someone else has bought it for you

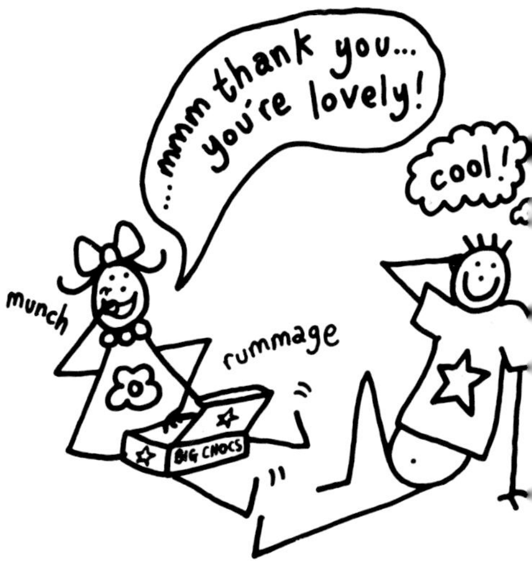
...mmm thank you... you're lovely!
cool!
munch
rummage
BIG CHOCS

a poem about being a
Chocoholic

My tummy sometimes
         talks to me

really don't know how

t says "I need some
              chocolate!

And I really need it now!"

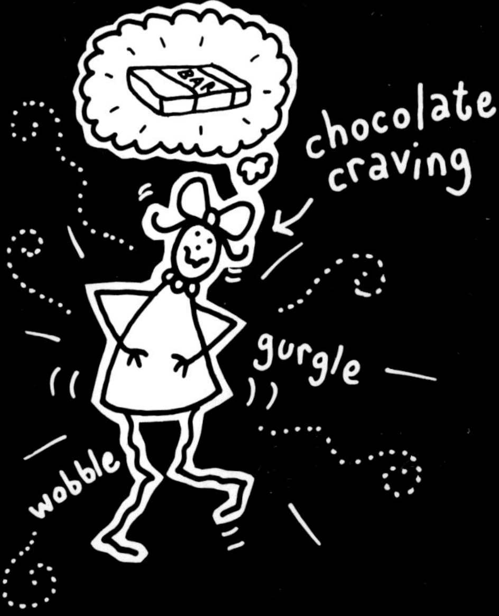
BAR
chocolate craving
gurgle
wobble

1st Rule of Chocolate

If you leave a tiny bit at the end, you can still persuade yourself that you haven't actually eaten a bar of chocolate

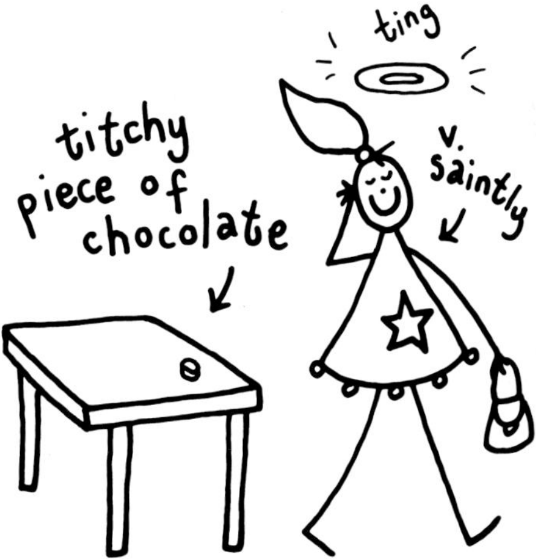
ting
titchy piece of chocolate
v. saintly

a poem about
Chocolate

When sensible people
see chocolate

They just think "fat thighs
and fat bum"

But all I can think of is
how it will taste

As it melts on the tip
of my tongue

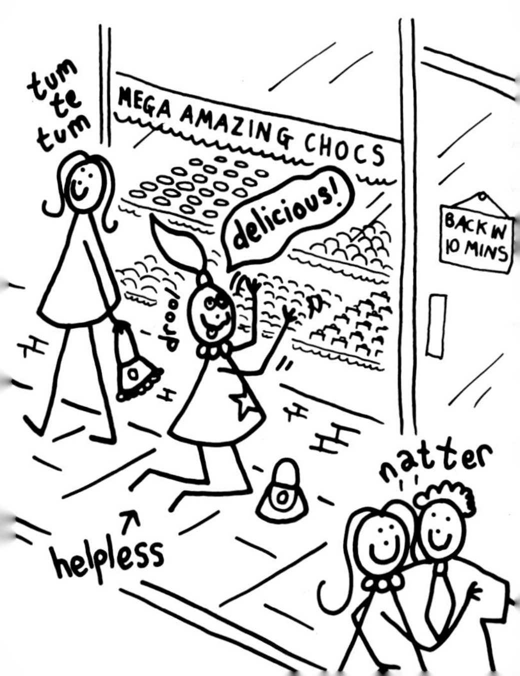
tum te tum
MEGA AMAZING CHOCS
delicious!
drool
BACK IN 10 MINS
natter
helpless

Warning:-

Sometimes chocolate can make you feel unbelievably frisky

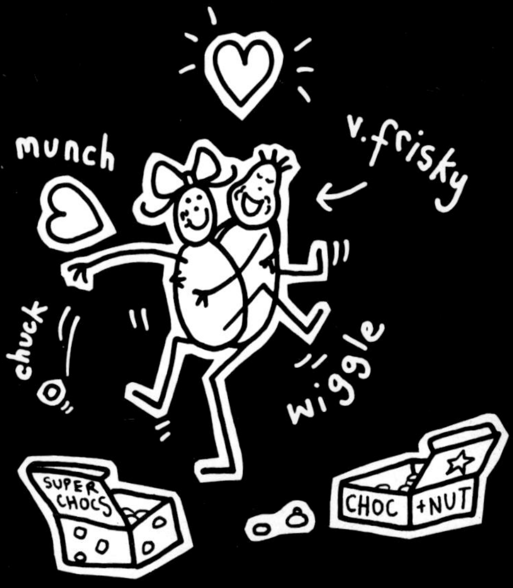
munch
v. frisky
chuck
wiggle
SUPER CHOCS
CHOC +NUT

a poem about

The Meaning of Life

Some people think that
  the Meaning of Life
Can be solved by some
   brainy machine
But I think I'd find it
By munching my way
Through a mountain of
  chocolate ice-cream

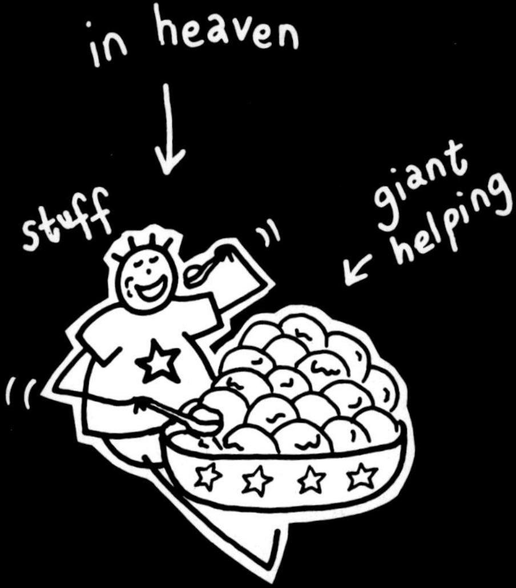
in heaven
stuff
giant helping

Chocolatey Thoughts

Sometimes even thinking about chocolate can make you feel happy all over

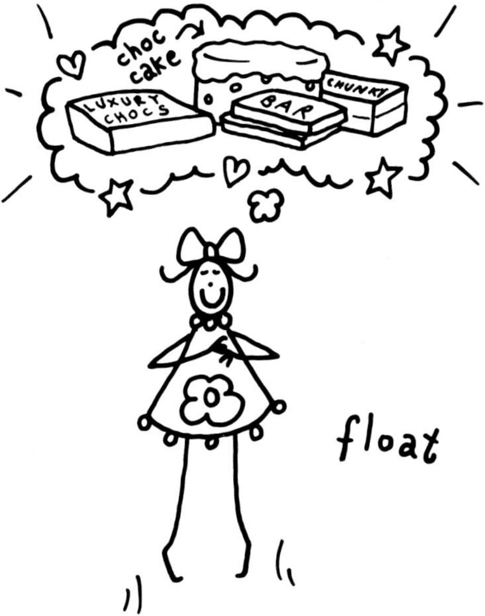
choc
cake
LUXURY
CHOCS
BAR
CHUNKY

float

a poem to say

I Love Chocolate

There's nothing I love
more than chocolate

Cos each time I take a
small bite

I just want to tear all
my clothes off

And feast on it naked
all night!

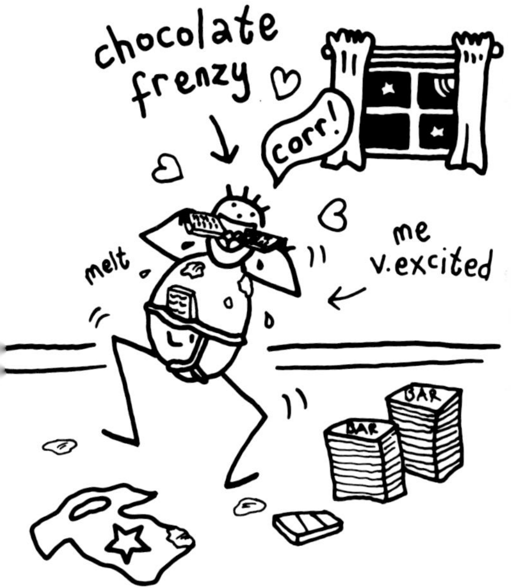
chocolate frenzy
corr!
me v.excited
melt
BAR
BAR

Chocolate and Boyfriends

Some girls think that chocolate is even better than boyfriends

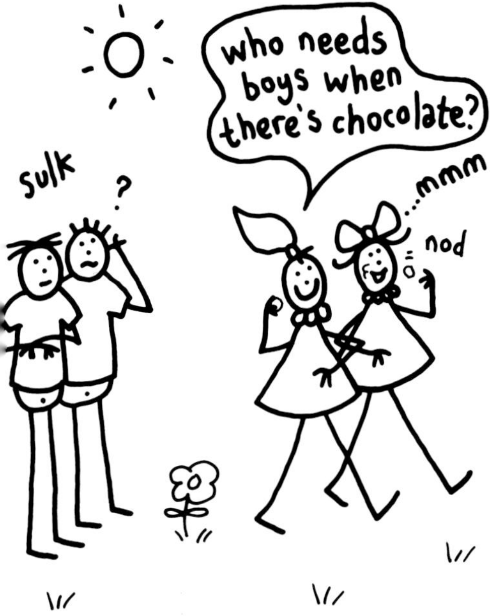
who needs boys when there's chocolate?
sulk
?
...mmm
nod

a poem about
Giving Up Chocolate

Some people give up
tobacco

And some give up alcohol too

But I think that giving
up chocolate

Is one thing I just
couldn't do

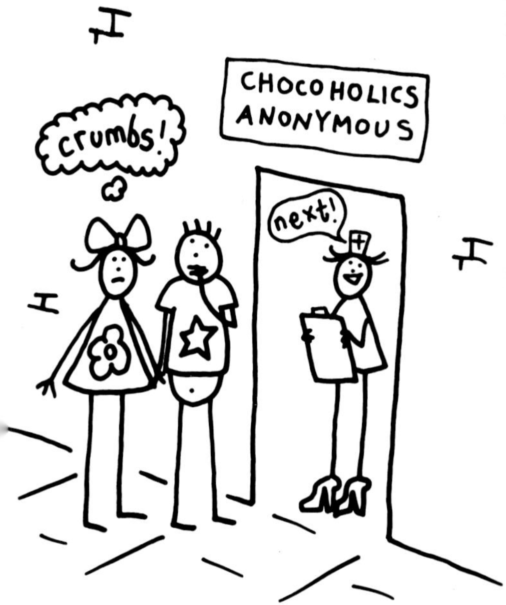

CHOCOHOLICS ANONYMOUS
crumbs!
next!

Mixed Chocolates

In mixed boxes of chocolates, why do they always put in a rubbish one that nobody wants to eat?

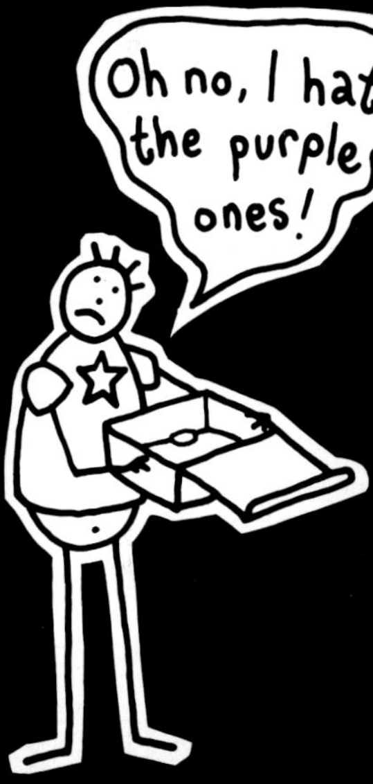
Oh no, I hate the purple ones!

a poem about
Chocolate Cake

Of all the fancy dishes

That a world class chef
can make

There's nothing that
will ever beat

A gooey chocolate cake!

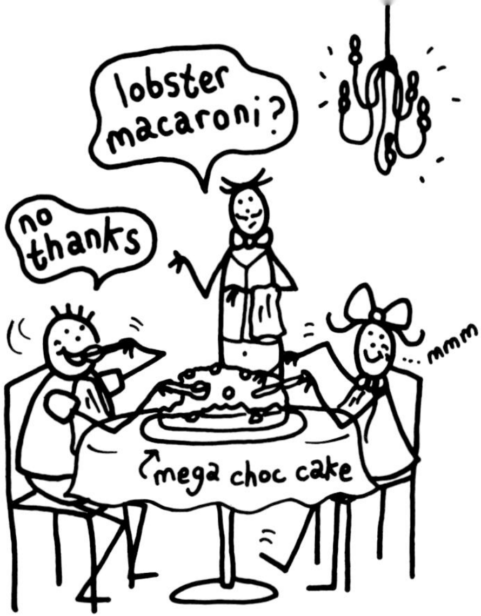
lobster macaroni?
no thanks
...mmm
mega choc cake

Beware:-

Some people's favourite fantasies involve using chocolate

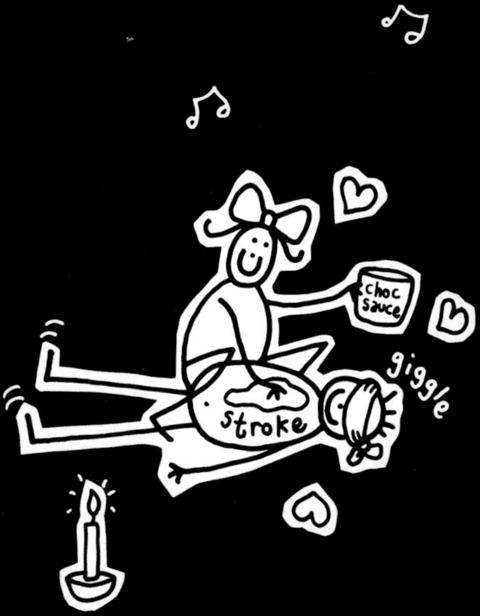
choc sauce
giggle
stroke

a poem about
Magic Chocolate

If someone invented a
chocolate

That actually made you
get thinner

They'd make a great
sackload of money

Cos that really would be
a winner!

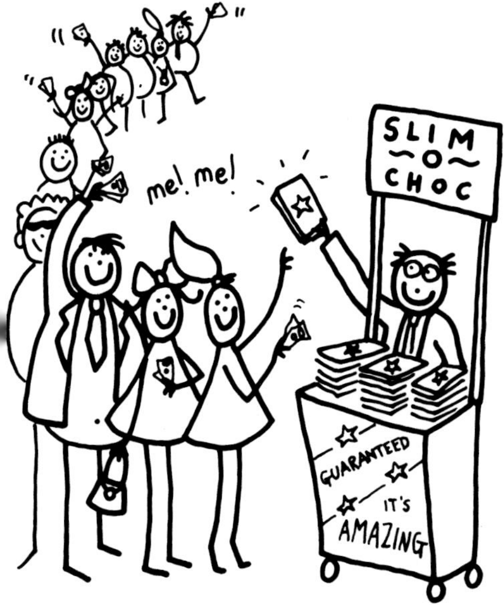
me! me!
SLIM ~O~ CHOC
GUARANTEED
IT'S
AMAZING

Special Tip

A little bit of chocolate before you move in for a snog can make your lips taste scrumptious

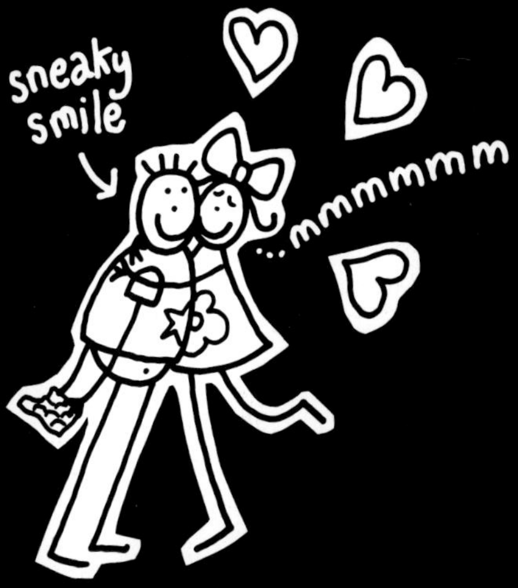
sneaky smile
...mmmmmm

a poem to say

I Love You

I want to tell you
something

Now at last I've found
a way

I love you more than
chocolate

And that's all I need
to say

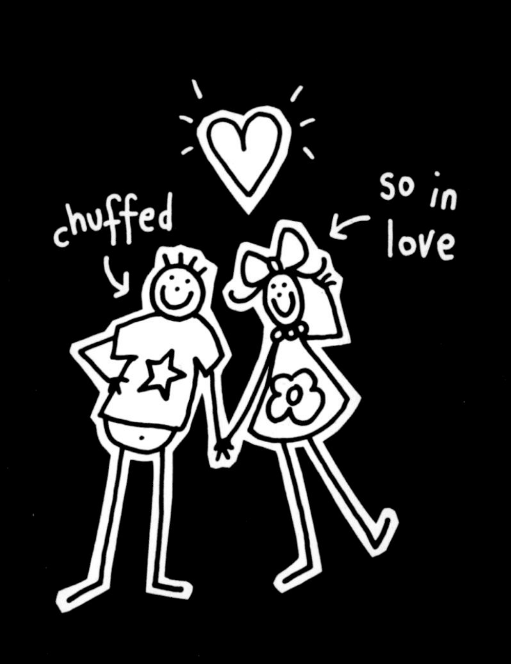
chuffed
so in love

2nd Rule of Chocolate

If you share a box of chocolates, nobody will actually know exactly who's had how many

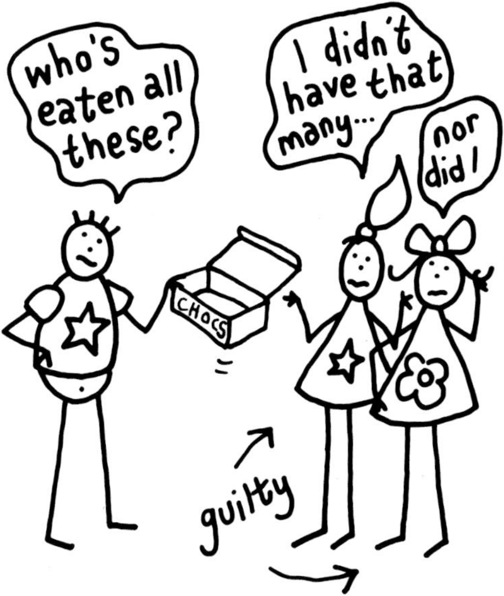
who's eaten all these?
I didn't have that many...
nor did I
CHOCS
guilty

a poem about
Hot Chocolate

Sometimes when life
seems all rotten

And people are doing my
head

I just make a mug of
hot chocolate

And snuggle up cosy
in bed

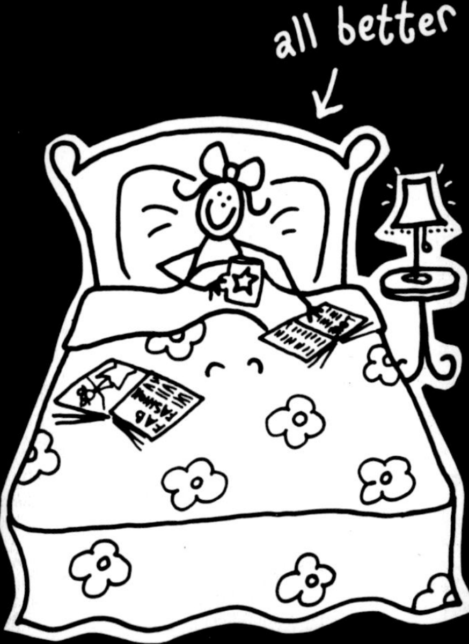
all better
FAB FASHION

Perfect Men

Perfect men know that there are times when only chocolate will do

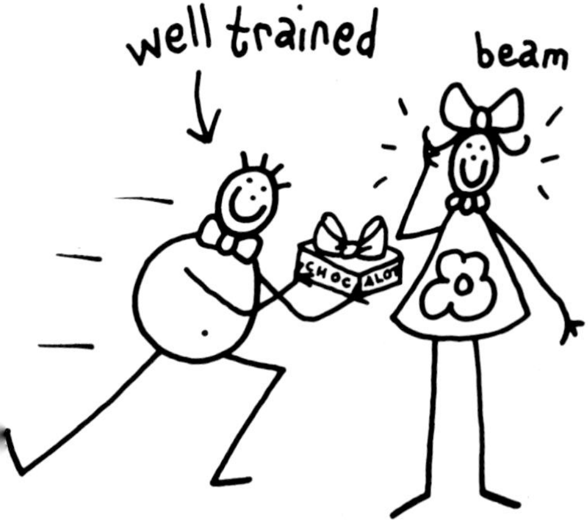
well trained
beam
CHOC
ALOT

a poem for a
Chocolate Queen

Eating loads of chocolate

Is your favourite ever
dream

So I think that we should
crown you

As the world's first
Chocolate Queen!

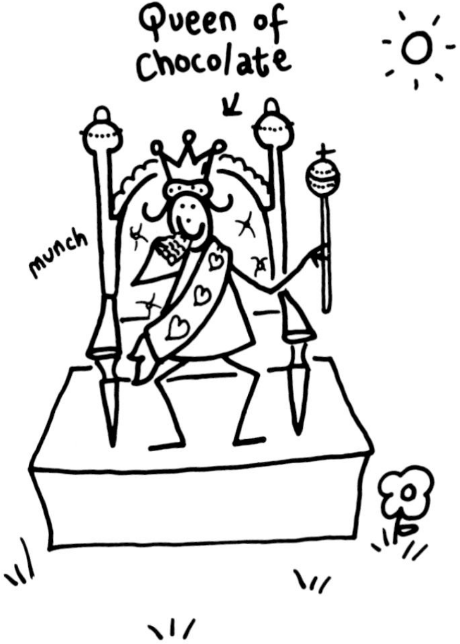
Queen of Chocolate
munch

<u>Warning</u> :-

People who don't like chocolate don't know how to have fun

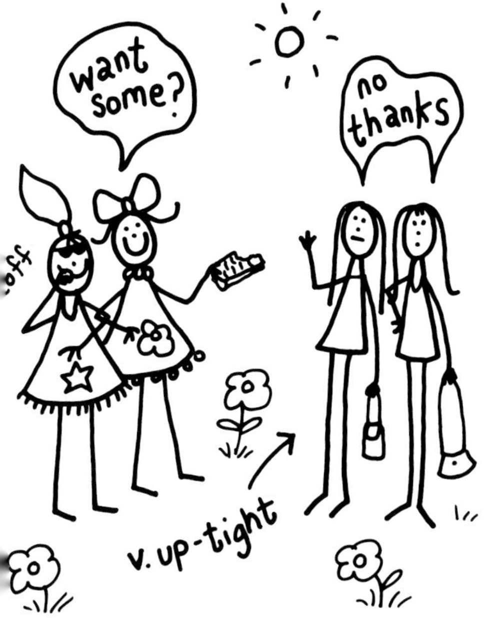
want some?
no thanks
v. up-tight

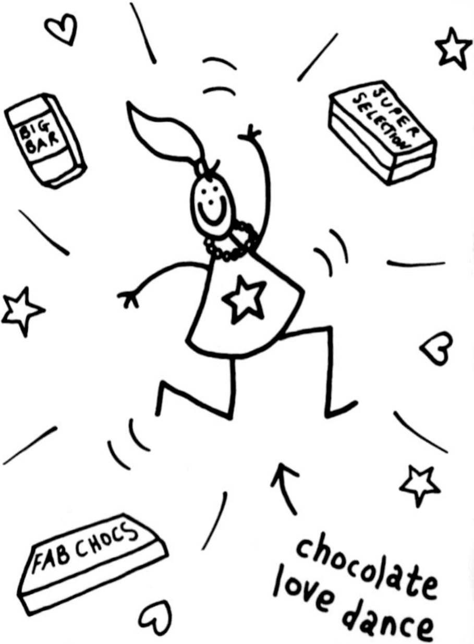

BIG BAR
SUPER SELECTION
FAB CHOCS
chocolate love dance